A FAMILY TREE

The information in
this book was lovingly
compiled by

_____

for

_____

date

_____

A FAMILY TREE
The history of our family

a Family Tree by norman rockwell

with illustrations by
Norman Rockwell

Design by
JMH Corporation
Indianapolis

Published by Craftique Productions, Inc.
Copyright © 1980 Creative Marketing Group, Inc.

Illustrations Copyright © The Curtis Publishing Company
1959, 1923, 1943, 1939, 1923, 1926, 1933, 1951,
1923, 1933, 1940, 1940, 1955, 1944, 1942, 1930.

Craftique Productions, Inc.
Westport, CT 06880
1100 Waterway Boulevard,
Indianapolis, IN 46202
ISBN: 0-86522-250-9
Printed in the United States of America.

Table of contents

The joys of genealogy

An introduction

Apirate on your family tree? A duke or an earl? It's not likely, nor is it likely that you will prove yourself heir to a fortune or gain an impressive coat of arms. The unknown-to-you ancestors that you discover when you become an amateur genealogist are almost certain to be farmers, small businessmen or craftsmen who lived and died in relative obscurity, either in the eastern U.S. or, if you go back further, in Europe. That's because most of the men and women who settled this continent were ordinary hard-working people, poor in purse but well endowed with energy and ambition. (Few pirates settled down to produce sons and daughters; few dukes and earls left the comforts of their ancestral estates to establish new homes in the American wilderness.)

Why bother, then, to find out who those ancestors were?

You will understand, once you begin family-tree-climbing.

When we seek out our ancestors we find much more than the cold, hard facts of names and dates, places of birth and burial.

Sometimes, if we are lucky, we find their faces in old photograph albums. Young faces, old faces, joyful or careworn, with styles of dress and posture that tell stories or pose questions.

(Look at the stripe down the sides of Great-Uncle Matthew's trousers—he must have been wearing part of the uniform he brought home from the Civil War! And Great-Aunt Ella's dress—isn't there a scrap of that material in Grandmother's comforter? Why, in old-time wedding pictures, did the *bride* always stand?)

More often than faces we find the names of our ancestors. We find them in courthouse record books, written in the spidery script of a long-dead clerk who may well have used a hand-cut goose quill in pokeberry ink. We find information about their weddings, because marriages, like births and deaths, are vital statistics preserved by county officials. We may also find descriptions of land they bought or sold and wills that contain fascinating lists of "goods and chattels" that tell us a great deal about how our ancestors lived.

Moving further afield, we find their names in records kept by the federal government. Old census lists. Homesteaders' claims. Muster rolls that list the names of all who served in the military, in all of our country's wars. We learn to what regiments they belonged, in which battles they fought. Still further back, the passenger lists of ships on which immigrants traveled to the New World have been collected and made available in reference books. If we find our ancestors' names on these lists, we will know in what years they sailed and from what ports in Europe.

And, in searching old cemeteries, we will find the names of our ancestors carved on thin, tall slabs of lichened stone that tilt a little, this way or that, from a century of frost-heavings. (How young, when she died! And the row of little stones marked "infant" beside hers—no names here. Did parents feel they were tempting fate when they named, too soon, the baby who faced so slender a chance for survival?)

These are the warp and woof of life, these gleanings from old books and maps and tombstones. Our personal stake in the American past, these snippets of information whet the appetite for more. Soon we are caught up in an exciting paper chase that is something like a crossword puzzle and something like a detective story. (Was the William G. who was wounded at Shiloh *our* William G.? He would have been the right age. And was our Jacob Hilgeshimer, buried in Pennsylvania, the one who came over on the *Jersey Star* in 1789?)

How to get started? A professional genealogist suggests the following steps:

1 Start with yourself and what you know about your parents and grandparents. Search family photo albums, family Bibles, old letters and diaries for more information. With each name list dates and places of birth and death, the name of wife or husband.

2 Talk to your relatives, especially the older ones, but be gentle and tactful. There may be family skeletons they are hesitant about discussing, or they may hate admitting they don't remember something. When writing to elderly relatives, send along self-addressed stamped envelopes for them to use in replying.

3 Check out the resources of the local library, the courthouse and the local historical society. Ask about old city directories, county histories and files of newspapers that may contain information about your ancestors.

4 The State Board of Health has birth and death records; the State Archives preserves land and military records; the State Library may have genealogist records of other families published in book form.

5 On the national level, the National Archives at Washington, D.C., preserves old census lists, military and immigration records. If you can't conveniently visit Washington, write them asking how to obtain information from them. You may also obtain useful information from the Daughters of the American Revolution headquarters in Washington and from the Mormon Church with headquarters at Salt Lake City, but with branch libraries and extensive microfilm resources in numerous locations around the country.

With luck, seemingly unrelated bits of information will fit together for you like bits of a jigsaw puzzle, forming pictures of your ancestors that are poignant, sometimes humorous, but always very human.

How to use this book

This book is planned as a link between past and future; between ancestors who are no longer living and descendents as yet unborn.

You are the only one who can forge this link. You do it by recording what you can learn of the past and what you want to preserve for the future.

The first section of this book is a "now" record. Write here the things you want to remember; things your grandchildren and great-grand-children will want to know. Record facts—like accurate birth dates and full names as they appear on birth certificates—but not *just* vital statistics. Write about the pets your home sheltered and the cars that were parts of your good times. Write about the funny things that happened and about the sad things. They are all parts of life . . . "Important Occasions" should include baptisms, christenings, confirmations, graduations and perhaps special honors granted to one member of the family or another. "Good Times to Remember" might include family reunions, wedding anniversaries and other events that bring together cousins, uncles and aunts as well as brothers and sisters. The "Other Information" pages are for the other things that you want to remember. One possibility: Assign a page to each child and let him or her describe (or picture) an event he wants remembered.

Chapters II and III provide an orderly system for recording basic information about the family's ancestors—names, dates and relationships. One chapter is for the male line, one for the female.

Begin by filling in parts of the Generational Charts with information you have now. On the single line at the left edge of the first chart write the full name of the father—the father of the family recorded on page 16. On the upper of the next two horizontal lines write his father's name,

and on the lower of the two horizontal lines, his mother's maiden name. Add dates and places of birth and, if deceased, dates and places of death. In the next part of the chart there are four lines for two family units—the father's grandparents—then eight lines for the great-grandparents. You will probably need help when you get this far; it will be time to start consulting older relatives, family Bibles and other sources.

Here are some rules genealogists follow when charting ancestors:

(1) Always use the full name rather than a nickname or initials.

(2) Always record a wife by her maiden or unmarried name, as this is the family name you will be tracing when you move back to the preceding generation.

(3) Use ink only if you are very sure of your information. As you go along you will find many errors and inconsistencies in the data you collect, much of it due to illegible handwriting or inaccurate copying at some time in the past. There's much to be said in favor of charting your ancestors in pencil that can be erased and changed when necessary.

The "family tree" charts in this book show five generations and go back about 150 years. You may never be able to fill in all the blanks on these two charts but, by contrast, you may be able to go much farther back in tracing some lines of the family. If so, you will need more Generational Charts. Draw them on some of the untitled pages, and start filling them in with more names and dates. The first name on the new chart should be the same as one of the last names on the old chart. Provide a cross-reference by writing "See page___" beside the name where it first appears.

The Family Charts provide space for Generational Charts—for example, the names of aunts and uncles, brothers and sisters. Be aware that each pair of names on the Generational Chart represents one family unit that could have a Family Chart. Identify a family with the husband's name and with an indication of the generation to which it belongs. The first Family Chart might be headed "The John Robert Smith Family, Father's (or Daddy's) Parents."

On the Family Charts, list all children in order of birth. If possible, tell what happened to each one—where they lived, whom they married, the names of their children. If you know a lot about these children you may wish to give them Family Chart pages of their own.

When listing deceased persons, it is well to give the name of the cemetery where they are buried as well as date and place of death.

If either of the parents married more than once, include the names of the second wife or husband along with the date of the death or divorce that ended the first marriage.

How many Family Charts you fill out will depend on how much information you accumulate about the various branches of the family. If you have only the names and dates for a married couple, you need not bother with a separate chart for them—their mention on the Generational Chart is enough. If you do acquire more information about the couple later, you can give them a Family Chart at that time. Untitled pages can be turned into Family Charts if you need more than are provided.

The rest of the book is yours to use as you wish. We suggest that you copy into it the actual source materials that refer to your ancestors. For example, when you find an entry from the 1860 Census that lists the members of an ancestor's household, with age and birthplace of each, copy all this onto one of the pages of Chapter IV (Where Our Ancestors Lived). A pension application filed by an ancestor who was a veteran of the War of 1812 might be copied onto one of the pages of Chapter VI (In War and Peace). The flowery phrases of an old marriage certificate and the church record of a baptism might go into Chapter V (Marriages, Births, Deaths). In each case, identify the source you copied from and give a date for it, and identify the person mentioned by adding a "See page—" note referring back to the Generational Chart on which his or her name first appears.

Chapter VIII ("I Remember . . .") may become the most valuable part of the book and the one you most enjoy creating. Here you can record stories that you heard the old folks tell when you were very young. Then coax your parents, grandparents and oldest relatives into telling you stories from their youth. They may even remember hearing stories about their grandparents' childhoods. As an oral historian, you will find a tape recorder useful because it allows you to transcribe and edit stories at your leisure. Copy the most interesting parts of these memories into Chapter VIII. Your grandchildren and great-grandchildren will thank you!

Before you begin your research, you may wish to obtain a free "Genie Kit" from the National Archives and Records Service (NNC), Washington, DC 20408. This kit provides information about the holdings of the National Archives, suggests basic tools for genealogical research, and is an excellent starting point for the novice genealogist.

Resource guide

Your best resource is the genealogical section of a local or state library. There you will find microfilm records, old county history books with biographical sketches of local residents, cemetery indexes that will help you locate ancestors' graves, old telephone books and city directories, even files of old newspapers. There you will also find trained librarians who will answer your questions and offer suggestions when you reach a blind alley in your research. A local historical society may also prove useful.

Pamphlets entitled "Where to Write for Birth and Death Records", "Where to Write for Marriage Records" and "Where to Write for Divorce Records" are available at no charge from The National Center for Health Statistics, 3700 East-West Highway, Rm. 157, Central Building, Hayattsville, MD 20782.

If an ancestor served as an U.S. Army officer in any war before 1917 or as an enlisted man before 1912, you can get a copy of his military and pension records by writing to The National Archives and Records Service, Central Reference Division, Washington, DC 20408. If an ancestor served in the U.S. Navy prior to 1885, only ships' logs are available for information. Naval records after 1885 are available from the Military Personnel Record Center, 9700 Page Boulevard, St. Louis, MO 63132. There you may also obtain records of Army officers after 1916 and enlisted personnel after 1912; all Naval officers after 1902; and all Marine personnel after 1895. All requests should include the full name of the veteran, the state from which he served and the period of time during which he served.

If an ancestor homesteaded land or was granted land because of his military service, the National Archives should have a record in the bounty-land application file. You will need to tell them the specific location of the land, including the name of the county and state, along with the approximate date of the land grant. You can also get a Cash Entry list of land bought from the Federal Domain.

The National Archives also has ships' passenger lists that include the names of many—but not all—of the immigrants who came to America from Europe after 1820. You will need to know the name of the ancestor who immigrated and the approximate date of his arrival in New York. Write the National Archives at the address given above and ask for the Official Request for Passenger Lists, a form you must use to request specific information.

For immigrants who became naturalized citizens after September 27, 1906, records of naturalization are available from the U.S. Immigration and Naturalization Office. 425 I Street, N.W., Washington, DC 20536. They include the name of the new citizen, the names of his spouse and children, along with the date of their arrival in this country. Records of naturalization prior to September 27, 1906 were not kept in a centralized location, but you may be able to obtain the information through state and local court records. (Keep in mind that these records exist only for immigrants who became naturalized citizens; many did not.)

Books you will find helpful:

American Society of Genealogists. *Genealogical Research: Methods and Sources.* 2 vols. Washington, DC, 1960, 1971.

Blockson, Charles L., with Ron Fry. *Black Genealogy.* Prentice-Hall, Inc., Englewood Cliffs, NJ, 1977.

Doane, Gilbert H. *Searching for Your Ancestors.* University of Minnesota Press, Minneapolis, MN, 1974.

Greenwood, Val D. *The Researcher's Guide to American Genealogy.* Genealogical Publishing Co., Inc., Baltimore, MD, 1977.

Linder, Bill R. *How to Trace Your Family History, A Basic Guide to Genealogy.* Everest House, New York, NY, 1978.

Pine, L. G. *The Genealogist's Encyclopedia.* Collier Books, A Division of Macmillan Publishing Co., New York, NY, 1969.

Rottenberg, Dad. *Finding Our Fathers, A Guidebook to Jewish Genealogy.* Random House, New York, NY, 1977.

I.
OUR FAMILY

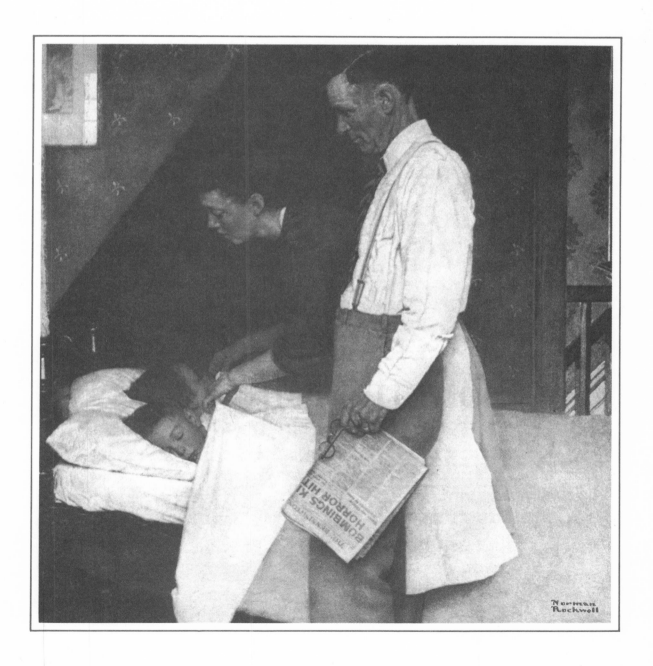

A record of today for tomorrow

Who we are

Father

Full name

Date of birth

Place of birth

Mother

Full name

Date of birth

Place of birth

Married

Date

Place

By

Witnesses or Attendants

Witnesses or Attendants

Children

Full name

Date of birth

Place of birth

Full name

Date of birth

Place of birth

Full name

Date of birth

Place of birth

Full name

Date of birth

Place of birth

Full name

Date of birth

Place of birth

Full name

Date of birth

Place of birth

Full name

Date of birth

Place of birth

Full name

Date of birth

Place of birth

Full name _____

Date of birth _____

Place of birth _____

Full name _____

Date of birth _____

Place of birth _____

Full name _____

Date of birth _____

Place of birth _____

Full name _____

Date of birth _____

Place of birth _____

About our family

Our homes

Address

From (date)   Until (date)

Description

Address

From (date)   Until (date)

Description

Address

From (date)   Until (date)

Description

Address

From (date)   Until (date)

Description

Address

From (date)   Until (date)

Description

Address

From (date)   Until (date)

Description

Address

From (date)   Until (date)

Description

Address

From (date)   Until (date)

Description

Address

From (date)   Until (date)

Description

Address

From (date)   Until (date)

Description

Our cars

Make _____ Model _____

Year _____ Color _____

Owned from (date) _____ Until (date) _____

Trips we took in this car _____

Things we will remember about this car _____

Make _____ Model _____

Year _____ Color _____

Owned from (date) _____ Until (date) _____

Trips we took in this car _____

Things we will remember about this car _____

Make _____ Model _____

Year _____ Color _____

Owned from (date) _____ Until (date) _____

Trips we took in this car _____

Things we will remember about this car _____

Make _____ Model _____

Year _____ Color _____

Owned from (date) _____ Until (date) _____

Trips we took in this car _____

Things we will remember about this car _____

Make _____ Model _____

Year _____ Color _____

Owned from (date) _____ Until (date) _____

Trips we took in this car _____

Things we will remember about this car _____

Make _____ Model _____

Year _____ Color _____

Owned from (date) _____ Until (date) _____

Trips we took in this car _____

Things we will remember about this car _____

Make _____ Model _____

Year _____ Color _____

Owned from (date) _____ Until (date) _____

Trips we took in this car _____

Things we will remember about this car _____

Make _____ Model _____

Year _____ Color _____

Owned from (date) _____ Until (date) _____

Trips we took in this car _____

Things we will remember about this car _____

Our pets

Name
_____

Breed or otner description
_____
_____
_____

From (date) _____ Until (date) _____

What we will remember about this pet
_____
_____
_____
_____
_____

Name
_____

Breed or other description
_____
_____
_____

From (date) _____ Until (date) _____

What we will remember about this pet
_____
_____
_____
_____
_____

Name
_____

Breed or other description
_____
_____
_____

From (date) _____ Until (date) _____

What we will remember about this pet
_____
_____
_____

Name
_____

Breed or other description
_____
_____
_____

From (date) _____ Until (date) _____

What we will remember about this pet
_____
_____
_____
_____
_____

Name
_____

Breed or other description
_____
_____
_____

From (date) _____ Until (date) _____

What we will remember about this pet
_____
_____
_____

Name
_____

Breed or other description
_____
_____
_____

From (date)   Until (date)
_____

What we will remember about this pet
_____
_____
_____
_____
_____

Name
_____

Breed or other description
_____
_____
_____

From (date)   Until (date)
_____

What we will remember about this pet
_____
_____
_____
_____
_____
_____

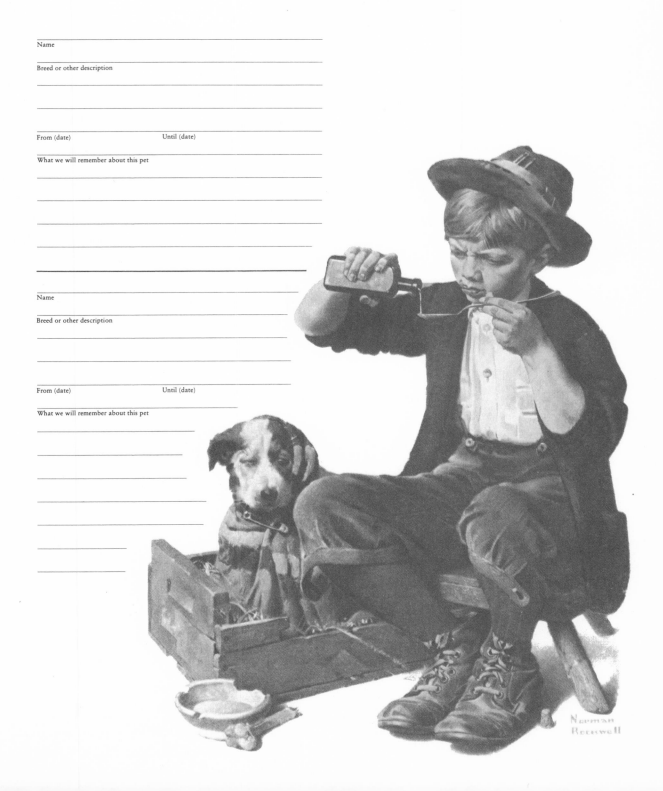

Important occasions

Date _____

Occasion _____

_____

Who was there _____

_____

_____

_____

_____

Date _____

Occasion _____

_____

Who was there _____

_____

_____

_____

_____

Date _____

Occasion _____

_____

Who was there _____

_____

_____

_____

_____

Date _____

Occasion _____

_____

Who was there _____

_____

_____

_____

Date _____

Occasion _____

_____

Who was there _____

_____

_____

Date _____

Occasion _____

_____

Who was there _____

_____

_____

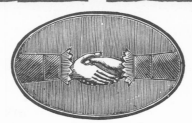

Date _____

Occasion _____
_____

Who was there _____
_____
_____
_____
_____

Date _____

Occasion _____
_____

Who was there _____
_____
_____
_____
_____

Date _____

Occasion _____
_____

Who was there _____
_____
_____
_____
_____

Date _____

Occasion _____
_____

Who was there _____
_____
_____
_____

Date _____

Occasion _____
_____

Who was there _____
_____
_____
_____
_____

Date _____

Occasion _____
_____

Who was there _____
_____
_____
_____
_____

Date _____

Occasion _____
_____

Who was there _____
_____
_____
_____
_____

Date _____

Occasion _____
_____

Who was there _____
_____
_____
_____

Good times
to remember

Other information

Other information

Family photographs

Family
photographs

II.
FATHER'S ANCESTRY

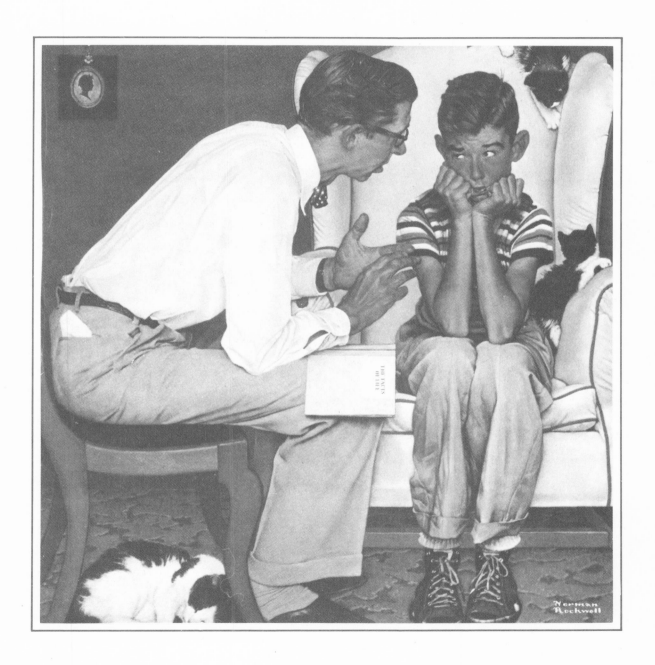

Forefathers and their forefathers

Generation chart

Father's grandparents

Is there more information about these persons on other pages of this book? If so, write "See page___" after the names.

Father's parents

Name

Born ___ Where

Died ___ Where

Name

Born ___ Where

Died ___ Where

Name

Born ___ Where

Died ___ Where

Name

Born ___ Where

Died ___ Where

Name

Born ___ Where

Died ___ Where

Name

Born ___ Where

Died ___ Where

His great-grandparents

His great-great-grandparents

Name

Born   Died

Name

Born   Died

Name

Born   Died

Name

Born   Died

Name

Born   Died

Name

Born   Died

Name

Born   Died

Name

Born   Died

Name

Born   Died

Name

Born   Died

Name

Born   Died

Name

Born   Died

Name

Born   Died

Name

Born   Died

Name

Born   Died

Name

Born   Died

Name

Born   Died

Name

Born   Died

Name

Born   Died

Name

Born   Died

Name

Born   Died

Name

Born   Died

Name

Born   Died

Name

Born   Died

Identify each family with the husband's name and the relationship. For example: The John Robert Smith Family, Father's parents. Whenever there is more information about a person elsewhere in this book, add "See page___" after the person's name.

The

Full name _____

Relationship _____

family

Husband's full name _____

Date of birth _____

Place _____

Date of death _____

Where buried _____

Date of marriage _____

Place _____

Business or profession _____

Place of residence _____

Wife's full name _____

Date of birth _____

Place _____

Date of death _____

Where buried _____

Was either married more than once? _____

_____

_____

Children

Name _____

Date of birth _____ Place _____

Date of death _____ Place of death or burial _____

Date of marriage _____ Spouse's name _____

Name _____

Date of birth _____ Place _____

Date of death _____ Place of death or burial _____

Date of marriage _____ Spouse's name _____

Name _____

Date of birth _____ Place _____

Date of death _____ Place of death or burial _____

Date of marriage _____ Spouse's name _____

Name _____

Date of birth _____ Place _____

Date of death _____ Place of death or burial _____

Date of marriage _____ Spouse's name _____

Name _____

Date of birth _____ Place _____

Date of death _____ Place of death or burial _____

Date of marriage _____ Spouse's name _____

Name _____

Date of birth _____ Place _____

Date of death _____ Place of death or burial _____

Date of marriage _____ Spouse's name _____

Name _____

Date of birth _____ Place _____

Date of death _____ Place of death or burial _____

Date of marriage _____ Spouse's name _____

Name _____

Date of birth _____ Place _____

Date of death _____ Place of death or burial _____

Date of marriage _____ Spouse's name _____

The

Full name _____   Relationship _____

family

Husband's full name _____   Wife's full name _____

Date of birth _____   Date of birth _____

Place _____   Place _____

Date of death _____   Date of death _____

Where buried _____   Where buried _____

Date of marriage _____   Was either married more than once? _____

Place _____

Business or profession _____

Place of residence _____

Children

Name _____   Name _____

Date of birth ___ Place ___   Date of birth ___ Place ___

Date of death ___ Place of death or burial ___   Date of death ___ Place of death or burial ___

Date of marriage ___ Spouse's name ___   Date of marriage ___ Spouse's name ___

Name _____   Name _____

Date of birth ___ Place ___   Date of birth ___ Place ___

Date of death ___ Place of death or burial ___   Date of death ___ Place of death or burial ___

Date of marriage ___ Spouse's name ___   Date of marriage ___ Spouse's name ___

Name _____   Name _____

Date of birth ___ Place ___   Date of birth ___ Place ___

Date of death ___ Place of death or burial ___   Date of death ___ Place of death or burial ___

Date of marriage ___ Spouse's name ___   Date of marriage ___ Spouse's name ___

Name _____   Name _____

Date of birth ___ Place ___   Date of birth ___ Place ___

Date of death ___ Place of death or burial ___   Date of death ___ Place of death or burial ___

Date of marriage ___ Spouse's name ___   Date of marriage ___ Spouse's name ___

The

Full name _____

Relationship _____

family

Husband's full name _____

Date of birth _____

Place _____

Date of death _____

Where buried _____

Date of marriage _____

Place _____

Business or profession _____

Place of residence _____

Wife's full name _____

Date of birth _____

Place _____

Date of death _____

Where buried _____

Was either married more than once? _____

_____

_____

_____

Children

Name _____

Date of birth _____ Place _____

Date of death _____ Place of death or burial _____

Date of marriage _____ Spouse's name _____

Name _____

Date of birth _____ Place _____

Date of death _____ Place of death or burial _____

Date of marriage _____ Spouse's name _____

Name _____

Date of birth _____ Place _____

Date of death _____ Place of death or burial _____

Date of marriage _____ Spouse's name _____

Name _____

Date of birth _____ Place _____

Date of death _____ Place of death or burial _____

Date of marriage _____ Spouse's name _____

Name _____

Date of birth _____ Place _____

Date of death _____ Place of death or burial _____

Date of marriage _____ Spouse's name _____

Name _____

Date of birth _____ Place _____

Date of death _____ Place of death or burial _____

Date of marriage _____ Spouse's name _____

Name _____

Date of birth _____ Place _____

Date of death _____ Place of death or burial _____

Date of marriage _____ Spouse's name _____

Name _____

Date of birth _____ Place _____

Date of death _____ Place of death or burial _____

Date of marriage _____ Spouse's name _____

The

Full name _____

Relationship _____

family

Husband's full name _____

Date of birth _____

Place _____

Date of death _____

Where buried _____

Date of marriage _____

Place _____

Business or profession _____

Place of residence _____

Wife's full name _____

Date of birth _____

Place _____

Date of death _____

Where buried _____

Was either married more than once? _____

Children

Name _____

Date of birth	Place

Date of death	Place of death or burial

Date of marriage	Spouse's name

Name _____

Date of birth	Place

Date of death	Place of death or burial

Date of marriage	Spouse's name

Name _____

Date of birth	Place

Date of death	Place of death or burial

Date of marriage	Spouse's name

Name _____

Date of birth	Place

Date of death	Place of death or burial

Date of marriage	Spouse's name

Name _____

Date of birth	Place

Date of death	Place of death or burial

Date of marriage	Spouse's name

Name _____

Date of birth	Place

Date of death	Place of death or burial

Date of marriage	Spouse's name

Name _____

Date of birth	Place

Date of death	Place of death or burial

Date of marriage	Spouse's name

The

Full name _____   Relationship _____

family

Husband's full name _____   Wife's full name _____

Date of birth _____   Date of birth _____

Place _____   Place _____

Date of death _____   Date of death _____

Where buried _____   Where buried _____

Date of marriage _____   Was either married more than once? _____

Place _____   _____

Business or profession _____   _____

Place of residence _____   _____

Children

Name _____   Name _____

Date of birth _____ Place _____   Date of birth _____ Place _____

Date of death _____ Place of death or burial _____   Date of death _____ Place of death or burial _____

Date of marriage _____ Spouse's name _____   Date of marriage _____ Spouse's name _____

Name _____   Name _____

Date of birth _____ Place _____   Date of birth _____ Place _____

Date of death _____ Place of death or burial _____   Date of death _____ Place of death or burial _____

Date of marriage _____ Spouse's name _____   Date of marriage _____ Spouse's name _____

Name _____   Name _____

Date of birth _____ Place _____   Date of birth _____ Place _____

Date of death _____ Place of death or burial _____   Date of death _____ Place of death or burial _____

Date of marriage _____ Spouse's name _____   Date of marriage _____ Spouse's name _____

Name _____   Name _____

Date of birth _____ Place _____   Date of birth _____ Place _____

Date of death _____ Place of death or burial _____   Date of death _____ Place of death or burial _____

Date of marriage _____ Spouse's name _____   Date of marriage _____ Spouse's name _____

The

Full name _____

Relationship _____

family

Husband's full name _____

Date of birth _____

Place _____

Date of death _____

Where buried _____

Date of marriage _____

Place _____

Business or profession _____

Place of residence _____

Wife's full name _____

Date of birth _____

Place _____

Date of death _____

Where buried _____

Was either married more than once? _____

Children

Name		Name	
Date of birth	Place	Date of birth	Place
Date of death	Place of death or burial	Date of death	Place of death or burial
Date of marriage	Spouse's name	Date of marriage	Spouse's name
Name		Name	
Date of birth	Place	Date of birth	Place
Date of death	Place of death or burial	Date of death	Place of death or burial
Date of marriage	Spouse's name	Date of marriage	Spouse's name
Name		Name	
Date of birth	Place	Date of birth	Place
Date of death	Place of death or burial	Date of death	Place of death or burial
Date of marriage	Spouse's name	Date of marriage	Spouse's name
Name		Name	
Date of birth	Place	Date of birth	Place
Date of death	Place of death or burial	Date of death	Place of death or burial
Date of marriage	Spouse's name	Date of marriage	Spouse's name

The

_____
Full name

_____
Relationship

family

Husband's full name	Wife's full name
Date of birth	Date of birth
Place	Place
Date of death	Date of death
Where buried	Where buried
Date of marriage	Was either married more than once?
Place	
Business or profession	
Place of residence	

Children

Name	Name
Date of birth — Place	Date of birth — Place
Date of death — Place of death or burial	Date of death — Place of death or burial
Date of marriage — Spouse's name	Date of marriage — Spouse's name
Name	Name
Date of birth — Place	Date of birth — Place
Date of death — Place of death or burial	Date of death — Place of death or burial
Date of marriage — Spouse's name	Date of marriage — Spouse's name
Name	Name
Date of birth — Place	Date of birth — Place
Date of death — Place of death or burial	Date of death — Place of death or burial
Date of marriage — Spouse's name	Date of marriage — Spouse's name
Name	Name
Date of birth — Place	Date of birth — Place
Date of death — Place of death or burial	Date of death — Place of death or burial
Date of marriage — Spouse's name	Date of marriage — Spouse's name

Other information

Other information

Other information

III.
MOTHER'S ANCESTRY

Grands, greats, and great-grands

Generation chart

Mother's grandparents

Is there more information about these persons on other pages of this book? If so, write "See page____" after the names.

Mother's parents

Name

Born   Where

Died   Where

Name

Born   Where

Died   Where

Name

Born   Where

Died   Where

Name

Born   Where

Died   Where

Name

Born   Where

Died   Where

Her great-grandparents

Her great-great-grandparents

Name

Born   Died

Name

Born   Died

Name

Born   Died

Name

Born   Died

Name

Born   Died

Name

Born   Died

Name

Born   Died

Name

Born   Died

Name

Born   Died

Name

Born   Died

Name

Born   Died

Name

Born   Died

Name

Born   Died

Name

Born   Died

Name

Born   Died

Name

Born   Died

Name

Born   Died

Name

Born   Died

Name

Born   Died

Name

Born   Died

Name

Born   Died

Identify each family with the husband's name and the relationship. For example: The John Robert Smith Family, Mother's parents. Whenever there is more information about a person elsewhere in this book, add "See page___" after the person's name.

The

_____   _____
Full name   Relationship

family

Husband's full name
_____

Date of birth
_____

Place
_____

Date of death
_____

Where buried
_____

Date of marriage
_____

Place
_____

Business or profession
_____

Place of residence
_____

Wife's full name
_____

Date of birth
_____

Place
_____

Date of death
_____

Where buried
_____

Was either married more than once?
_____

_____

_____

_____

Children

Name
_____

Date of birth	Place

Date of death	Place of death or burial

Date of marriage	Spouse's name

Name
_____

Date of birth	Place

Date of death	Place of death or burial

Date of marriage	Spouse's name

Name
_____

Date of birth	Place

Date of death	Place of death or burial

Date of marriage	Spouse's name

Name
_____

Date of birth	Place

Date of death	Place of death or burial

Date of marriage	Spouse's name

Name
_____

Date of birth	Place

Date of death	Place of death or burial

Date of marriage	Spouse's name

Name
_____

Date of birth	Place

Date of death	Place of death or burial

Date of marriage	Spouse's name

Name
_____

Date of birth	Place

Date of death	Place of death or burial

Date of marriage	Spouse's name

Name
_____

Date of birth	Place

Date of death	Place of death or burial

Date of marriage	Spouse's name

The

_____
Full name

_____
Relationship

family

Husband's full name
_____

Date of birth
_____

Place
_____

Date of death
_____

Where buried
_____

Date of marriage
_____

Place
_____

Business or profession
_____

Place of residence
_____

_____

Wife's full name
_____

Date of birth
_____

Place
_____

Date of death
_____

Where buried
_____

Was either married more than once?
_____

_____

_____

_____

Children

Name
_____

Date of birth	Place
Date of death	Place of death or burial
Date of marriage	Spouse's name

Name
_____

Date of birth	Place
Date of death	Place of death or burial
Date of marriage	Spouse's name

Name
_____

Date of birth	Place
Date of death	Place of death or burial
Date of marriage	Spouse's name

Name
_____

Date of birth	Place
Date of death	Place of death or burial
Date of marriage	Spouse's name

Name
_____

Date of birth	Place
Date of death	Place of death or burial
Date of marriage	Spouse's name

Name
_____

Date of birth	Place
Date of death	Place of death or burial
Date of marriage	Spouse's name

Name
_____

Date of birth	Place
Date of death	Place of death or burial
Date of marriage	Spouse's name

Name
_____

Date of birth	Place
Date of death	Place of death or burial
Date of marriage	Spouse's name

The

Full name _____

Relationship _____

family

Husband's full name _____	Wife's full name _____
Date of birth _____	Date of birth _____
Place _____	Place _____
Date of death _____	Date of death _____
Where buried _____	Where buried _____
Date of marriage _____	Was either married more than once? _____
Place _____	_____
Business or profession _____	_____
Place of residence _____	_____

Children

Name _____		Name _____	
Date of birth _____	Place _____	Date of birth _____	Place _____
Date of death _____	Place of death or burial _____	Date of death _____	Place of death or burial _____
Date of marriage _____	Spouse's name _____	Date of marriage _____	Spouse's name _____
Name _____		Name _____	
Date of birth _____	Place _____	Date of birth _____	Place _____
Date of death _____	Place of death or burial _____	Date of death _____	Place of death or burial _____
Date of marriage _____	Spouse's name _____	Date of marriage _____	Spouse's name _____
Name _____		Name _____	
Date of birth _____	Place _____	Date of birth _____	Place _____
Date of death _____	Place of death or burial _____	Date of death _____	Place of death or burial _____
Date of marriage _____	Spouse's name _____	Date of marriage _____	Spouse's name _____
Name _____		Name _____	
Date of birth _____	Place _____	Date of birth _____	Place _____
Date of death _____	Place of death or burial _____	Date of death _____	Place of death or burial _____
Date of marriage _____	Spouse's name _____	Date of marriage _____	Spouse's name _____

The

_____   _____
Full name   Relationship

family

_____   _____
Husband's full name   Wife's full name

_____   _____
Date of birth   Date of birth

_____   _____
Place   Place

_____   _____
Date of death   Date of death

_____   _____
Where buried   Where buried

_____   _____
Date of marriage   Was either married more than once?

_____   _____
Place

_____   _____
Business or profession

_____   _____
Place of residence

Children

_____   _____
Name   Name

_____ _____   _____ _____
Date of birth   Place   Date of birth   Place

_____ _____   _____ _____
Date of death   Place of death or burial   Date of death   Place of death or burial

_____ _____   _____ _____
Date of marriage   Spouse's name   Date of marriage   Spouse's name

_____   _____
Name   Name

_____ _____   _____ _____
Date of birth   Place   Date of birth   Place

_____ _____   _____ _____
Date of death   Place of death or burial   Date of death   Place of death or burial

_____ _____   _____ _____
Date of marriage   Spouse's name   Date of marriage   Spouse's name

_____   _____
Name   Name

_____ _____   _____ _____
Date of birth   Place   Date of birth   Place

_____ _____   _____ _____
Date of death   Place of death or burial   Date of death   Place of death or burial

_____ _____   _____ _____
Date of marriage   Spouse's name   Date of marriage   Spouse's name

_____   _____
Name   Name

_____ _____   _____ _____
Date of birth   Place   Date of birth   Place

_____ _____   _____ _____
Date of death   Place of death or burial   Date of death   Place of death or burial

_____ _____   _____ _____
Date of marriage   Spouse's name   Date of marriage   Spouse's name

The

Full name _____   Relationship _____

family

Husband's full name _____   Wife's full name _____

Date of birth _____   Date of birth _____

Place _____   Place _____

Date of death _____   Date of death _____

Where buried _____   Where buried _____

Date of marriage _____   Was either married more than once? _____

Place _____

Business or profession _____

Place of residence _____

Children

Name _____   Name _____

Date of birth _____ Place _____   Date of birth _____ Place _____

Date of death _____ Place of death or burial _____   Date of death _____ Place of death or burial _____

Date of marriage _____ Spouse's name _____   Date of marriage _____ Spouse's name _____

Name _____   Name _____

Date of birth _____ Place _____   Date of birth _____ Place _____

Date of death _____ Place of death or burial _____   Date of death _____ Place of death or burial _____

Date of marriage _____ Spouse's name _____   Date of marriage _____ Spouse's name _____

Name _____   Name _____

Date of birth _____ Place _____   Date of birth _____ Place _____

Date of death _____ Place of death or burial _____   Date of death _____ Place of death or burial _____

Date of marriage _____ Spouse's name _____   Date of marriage _____ Spouse's name _____

Name _____   Name _____

Date of birth _____ Place _____   Date of birth _____ Place _____

Date of death _____ Place of death or burial _____   Date of death _____ Place of death or burial _____

Date of marriage _____ Spouse's name _____   Date of marriage _____ Spouse's name _____

The

Full name _____

Relationship _____

family

Husband's full name _____	Wife's full name _____
Date of birth _____	Date of birth _____
Place _____	Place _____
Date of death _____	Date of death _____
Where buried _____	Where buried _____
Date of marriage _____	Was either married more than once? _____
Place _____	_____
Business or profession _____	_____
Place of residence _____	_____

Children

Name _____

Date of birth _____	Place _____
Date of death _____	Place of death or burial _____
Date of marriage _____	Spouse's name _____

Name _____

Date of birth _____	Place _____
Date of death _____	Place of death or burial _____
Date of marriage _____	Spouse's name _____

Name _____

Date of birth _____	Place _____
Date of death _____	Place of death or burial _____
Date of marriage _____	Spouse's name _____

Name _____

Date of birth _____	Place _____
Date of death _____	Place of death or burial _____
Date of marriage _____	Spouse's name _____

Name _____

Date of birth _____	Place _____
Date of death _____	Place of death or burial _____
Date of marriage _____	Spouse's name _____

Name _____

Date of birth _____	Place _____
Date of death _____	Place of death or burial _____
Date of marriage _____	Spouse's name _____

Name _____

Date of birth _____	Place _____
Date of death _____	Place of death or burial _____
Date of marriage _____	Spouse's name _____

Name _____

Date of birth _____	Place _____
Date of death _____	Place of death or burial _____
Date of marriage _____	Spouse's name _____

The

_____ _____
Full name   Relationship

family

Husband's full name _____ Wife's full name _____

Date of birth _____ Date of birth _____

Place _____ Place _____

Date of death _____ Date of death _____

Where buried _____ Where buried _____

Date of marriage _____ Was either married more than once? _____

Place _____ _____

Business or profession _____ _____

Place of residence _____ _____

_____ _____

Children

Name _____ Name _____

Date of birth _____ Place _____ Date of birth _____ Place _____

Date of death _____ Place of death or burial _____ Date of death _____ Place of death or burial _____

Date of marriage _____ Spouse's name _____ Date of marriage _____ Spouse's name _____

Name _____ Name _____

Date of birth _____ Place _____ Date of birth _____ Place _____

Date of death _____ Place of death or burial _____ Date of death _____ Place of death or burial _____

Date of marriage _____ Spouse's name _____ Date of marriage _____ Spouse's name _____

Name _____ Name _____

Date of birth _____ Place _____ Date of birth _____ Place _____

Date of death _____ Place of death or burial _____ Date of death _____ Place of death or burial _____

Date of marriage _____ Spouse's name _____ Date of marriage _____ Spouse's name _____

Name _____ Name _____

Date of birth _____ Place _____ Date of birth _____ Place _____

Date of death _____ Place of death or burial _____ Date of death _____ Place of death or burial _____

Date of marriage _____ Spouse's name _____ Date of marriage _____ Spouse's name _____

Other information

Other information

Other information

IV.
WHERE OUR
ANCESTORS LIVED

Census records,
old phone books, city directories

V.
MARRIAGES, BIRTHS, DEATHS

Courthouse, state and church records

VI.
WAR AND PEACE

Military records

VII.
"DEAR DIARY"

Letters and diaries

VIII.
"I REMEMBER..."

Oral tradition